Jobs

Written by Sandra Iversen

Von has a job.
What is it?

Von

Pop has a job.
What is it?

Pop

Don has a job.
What is it?

Don

Bob has a job.
What is it?